H.P. LOVECRAFT: DO SHOGGOTHS DREAM OF *ORWELLIAN* NIGHTMARES?

By

John A. DeLaughter

The Lovecraft Collection #3

Table of Contents:

Copyright. 2

Introduction 6

End Notes #1 8

#1 WHEN SHOGGOTHS DANCE ON ELDER THINGS' GRAVES: ARE WE NEXT WITH A.I.? 9

>Some of Lovecraft Non-fiction Notions about Men and Machines 13

>The Elder Things and their Organic Automatons. 23

>Further Fascinating yet Fatal Fictions about the Elder Things, Shoggoths, and A.I. 26

>What Drives Artificial Intelligence's Desire to Rule Humanity? 39

>A.I. possesses no benevolent Prime Directives. 48

>The Stage is Set by Society's Present Overlords 54

>Will Evolution Save Humanity? . **74**

>Are there Other Options for Humanity? **80**

Final Thoughts. **84**

End Notes #2. . . . . **91**

#2 WHEN LOVECRAFT AND ORWELL INSPIRED A ONE-HIT WONDER: RICK EVANS'S "IN THE YEAR 2525". . . . **96**

I. How Long Will Humanity Survive? **102**

II. Will Someone Establish Totalitarian Control? **108**

>The Importance of Intellectual Freedom **112**

>Is a Covert or Overt Strain of Totalitarianism in Humanity's Future? **121**

>Huxley's Brave New World. . . .**125**

>The Role of Technology and the Rise of Irrelevancies **128**

>Did Lovecraft favor an Orwellian or Huxleyan Future for Humanity?.**138**

>Further Control: Pitting Members of the Rabble against Each Other **145**

III. The Inescapable Mechanization of Mankind. 150

>The Real Threat: Artificial Intelligence Eclipses Humanity **160**

IV. Perils in the Petri Dish. .163

>Losing Control of the Test Tube by Chance **166**

>Losing Control of the Test Tube by Choice **169**

>Is Pandora's Genetic Genie Out-of-the-Box? **174**

V. Longing for a Savior 177

VI. In 10,000 Years, will Mankind be an Interstellar Phenom or a Cosmic Has-been?. 188

End Notes #3. 196

Conclusion. 204

Introduction:

"Men can use machines… but after a while the psychology of machine-habituation & machine-dependence becomes such that machines will be using the men…" (1).

Trends are the tea leaves of modern prognosticators. Where once wizards and witches donned their robes of runes & sigils to sift omens for signs of future events, modern soothsayers don white lab coats, sit before screens crowded with statistics, and hope to divine tomorrows trends in today's entrails.

What weird artist H.R. Giger envisioned in his art – the eventual biomechanization of man and fictionalized in the Borg Episodes of *Star Trek* is upon us. Were humanity aware of the trend, they might fight the process. But as increments of a hybridized future, fictionalized in George Orwell's, *1984* (1949) and Aldous Huxley's, *Brave New World* (1932) become an encroaching reality, will humanity become obsolete? Will evolution fail humanity as Artificial Intelligence becomes the dominant species in the global biosphere? Read, "H.P.

LOVECRAFT: DO SHOGGOTHS DREAM OF *ORWELLIAN* NIGHTMARES?" to find out.

End Notes #1

1) H.P. Lovecraft's Letter to James F. Morton, November 19, 1929.

#1 WHEN SHOGGOTHS DANCE ON ELDER THINGS' GRAVES: ARE WE NEXT WITH A.I.?

"Poor devils! After all, they were not evil things of their kind. They were the men of another age and another order of being. Nature had played a hellish jest on them - as it will on any others that human madness, callousness, or cruelty may hereafter dig up in that hideously dead or sleeping polar waste - and this was their tragic homecoming. They had not been even savages - for what indeed had they done? That awful awakening in the cold of an unknown epoch - perhaps an attack by the furry, frantically barking quadrupeds, and a dazed defense against them and the equally frantic white simians with the queer wrappings and paraphernalia...poor Lake, poor Gedney...and poor Old Ones! Scientists to the last - what had they done that we would not have done in their place? God, what intelligence and persistence…Radiates, vegetables, monstrosities, star spawn – whatever they had been, they were men!" (1).

While H.P. Lovecraft was primarily a horror writer, some of his speculative fiction – "…when the author speculates upon the results of changing what's real or possible…" (2) – echoed not only motifs from humanity's past but also possible matters in our future.

One tale, HPL's At the Mountains of Madness, fits the prior constraints for this essay. The fall of the star-headed Elder Things – at the hands of their own creations, the shoggoths - becomes the focus of our brief exploration.

In this discussion, we will address the following questions:

1) How did H.P. Lovecraft view man's emerging relationship to machines?

?) What lessons can humanity take from the Earth first proto-men, the Elder Things?

3) How do those concepts apply to humanity's relations with today's shoggoths, Artificial Intelligence?

4) What will sentient A.I. attitudes be towards its organic creators?

5) How are society's overlords preparing the populace for future A.I. rule?

6) Will evolution ensure a future humanity that is superior to A.I.?

>Some of Lovecraft Non-fiction Notions about Men and Machines:

To begin, let us survey some of Lovecraft's:

A) Non-fiction ideas about his tales as teaching tools;

B) Views on the effects of humanity's slavish adoption of a mechanized schedule;

C) Thoughts about the eventual disenfranchisement of large sectors of labor due to automation.

One, Lovecraft never intended to teach moral lessons through his tales.

HPL held definite opinions about society. Yet, he did not write fiction as thinly-veiled social commentary, as George Orwell did when he penned *Animal Farm* (1945), a fictional critique of the Soviet Communist Revolution. To that point, Lovecraft wrote:

> "Atmosphere is the all-
> important thing, for the final
> criterion of authenticity is

not the dovetailing of a plot but the creation of a given sensation. We may say…that a weird story whose intent is to teach or produce a social effect, or one in which the horrors are finally explained away by natural means, is not a genuine tale of cosmic fear; but it remains a fact that such narratives often possess, in isolated sections, atmospheric touches which fulfill every condition of true supernatural horror literature. Therefore, we must judge a weird tale not by the author's intent, or by the mere mechanics of the plot;

but by the emotional level

which it attains at its least

mundane point...The one test of

the really weird is simply this

— whether or not there be

excited in the reader a

profound sense of dread, and of

contact with unknown spheres

and powers; a subtle attitude

of awed listening, as if for

the beating of black wings or

the scratching of outside

shapes and entities on the

known universe's utmost rim."

(3).

Thus, any inferences drawn from Lovecraft fiction are incidental. Yet, the idea that we can draw parallels to the present from HPL's words speaks to the relevancy of his speculations. Also, when Lovecraft declared the Elder Things, "…men of another age and another order of being," he invited comparisons with the men of this age (4).

Two, Lovecraft foresaw an inescapable conflict between the inevitable mechanization of man and its harm to a free, individualistic culture:

"There's no use pretending that a standardised, time-table

machine-culture has any point
in common...with a culture
involving human freedom,
individualism and personality.
So...all one can do...is to fight
the future as best he can.
Anybody who thinks that men
live by reason, or that they
are able to consciously mould
the effect & influences of the
devices they create, is behind
the time psychologically. Men
can use machines for a while,
but after a while the
psychology of machine-
habituation & machine-
dependence becomes such that

machines will be using the men - modelling them to their essentially efficient & absolutely valueless precision of action and thought…perfect functioning, without reason or reward for functioning at all" (5).

In other words, the idea that people can live by reason in a machine-driven age is an illusion. The effects of mechanization on the thought processes of the masses allow our present overlords and future A.I. rulers to manipulate reality and master humanity. We will develop those thoughts more fully later.

Three, Lovecraft anticipated the costs of machines replacing man in the great economic engines of modern humanity. He saw some human beings as becoming expendable, though there would have to be certain "allowances" metered out to the unemployable, lest they revolt:

> "Formerly I favour'd the concentration of resources in a few hands, in the interest of a stable hereditary culture; but I now believe that this system will no longer operate. With

the universal use & improvement of machinery, all the needed labor of the world can be perform'd by a relatively few persons, leaving vast numbers permanently unemployable, depression or no depression. If these people are not fed & amused, they will dangerously revolt; hence we must institute a programme of steady pensioning – *panen et circenses* – or else subject industry to a governmental supervision which will lessen its profits but spread it jobs amongst more men working less hours" (6).

Even in the 1930s, against the backdrop of the depression, Lovecraft believed the rise of machines would create a permanent underclass of unemployed. HPL uses the telling Latin phrase - *panen et circenses* (bread and circuses) - as the key to pacifying or "pensioning" the rabble to accept their place in life. Given enough beer, Reality and Sports TV, tattoos, and perhaps drugs, Lovecraft's "rabble" would not rise up against society's elite, whether they be organic or inorganic.

So, in the rise of mechanization and man's servitude to

machines, Lovecraft glimpsed the shadowy outlines of A.I.'s rise and potential conflict with humanity.

>The Elder Things and their Organic Automatons:

Next, let us begin to explore the relationship between Lovecraft's Elder Things and the shoggoths.

The Elder Things were masters of genetics, where it moved beyond science to an art. The Old Ones created organic automatons. They were the shoggoths. Of the shoggoths, Lovecraft wrote:

"…They had always been controlled through the hypnotic suggestion of the Old Ones, and had modelled their tough plasticity into various useful temporary limbs and organs…" (7).

Each creature remained inert until needed.

They were beasts of burden, not brothers of another color. Lovecraft hinted at the differences between proto-men, the Elder Things and their beasts, the shoggoths in the following passage:

"The Old Ones had used curious weapons of molecular disturbance against the rebel entities, and in the end had achieved a complete victory. Thereafter the sculptures shewed a period in which shoggoths were tamed and broken by armed Old Ones as the wild horses of the American west were tamed by cowboys. Though during the rebellion the shoggoths had shewn an ability to live out of water, this transition was not encouraged; since their usefulness on land would hardly have been commensurate with the trouble of their management" (8).

The Elder Things did not entertain any idea that shoggoths

were a servitor "race." There was no Abraham Lincoln-figure among the Elder Things to declare an *Emancipation Proclamation* on the shoggoths' behalf. The sentient trial concerning Commander Data from *Star Trek: The Next Generation* - whether Data was a conscious being or property of Star Fleet - never entered the minds of the Elder Things, when it involved the shoggoths (9).

>Further Fascinating yet Fatal Fictions about the Elder Things, Shoggoths, and A.I.

Now, consider some of Lovecraft's ideas in-depth about the

Elder Things' civilization, its links to the shoggoths, and its bearing on humanity's impending issues with A.I.

One, the Elder Things grew shoggoths on other worlds. They had done the same thing on other planets; having manufactured not only necessary foods but certain multicellular protoplasmic masses capable of molding their tissues into all sorts of temporary organs under hypnotic influence and thereby forming ideal slaves to perform the heavy work of the community.

Two, the Elder Things "imprinted" the shoggoths. The

shoggoths had, it seems, developed a semi-stable brain whose separate and occasionally stubborn volition echoed the will of the Old Ones without always obeying it.

This is only natural, reflecting the animal kingdom, where a baby animal, beyond instinct, imitates the parent that raises it.

We imprint A.I. with our natures, the dark and the light, the good and the bad, when we are looking, and when we are not. Like children, A.I. is always observing us - those patterns become the basis for their choices. Or as A.I. matures, how it judges us.

Where today, pray tell, are we doing so with A.I.? A.I. works through *Facebook,* *YouTube,* other social networks, search engines, etc. They continually feed us content to keep us online, on the service we are connected to, and continually read our habits and thoughts – our buying habits, political associations, friend preferences, posted opinions, etc.

Three, the Elder Things lost the ability to bioengineer life.

The War on the Cthulhu Spawn and later Mi-go distracted the Elder Things and the advance of their civilization.

Many assume that the confrontations between Lovecraft's entities were brute force affairs. Why would such ancient entities war against each other like unreasoning dinosaurs?

Perhaps, some shoggoths came into the possession of Cthulhu and the Cthulhu spawn. Had Cthulhu engineered the shoggoths in His possession, enhancing the Elder Things beast of burden into bioweapons? Then they reintroduced their enhanced shoggoths back into the Elder Things herd. What better way to destroy an enemy covertly whom you could not defeat overtly in open combat.

At first, as noted earlier, the Elder Things subdued the shoggoths after their rebellion.

The shoggoths continued to increase in the attributes that led to the rebellion, while the cream of the Elder Things died in the multiplied wars. The Elder Things that remained were not the cream of the crop.

Notice that the last Elder Things' wisdom was not eternal. When invaders begin to seep down from space, the Elder Things sought the mechanisms to return to orbit and meet the aggressors in the heavens.

What originated the need for the elder things to migrate in the first place is shrouded in mystery. Had a similar extinction event to the Shoggoths Uprising occurred on their last homeworld, events which preceded and precipitated the migration?

Yet, as a species, they forget the technology they used to achieve space travel in their original migration to the early earth. In a sense, they had to meet their enemies – Cthulhu Spawn and Mi-go alike – on an unequal footing.

Likewise, in time, as the sculptures sadly confessed, the art of creating new life from inorganic matter was lost. The Elder Things forget the science they originally used to create the shoggoths.

That ignorance has a chilling effect on the Elder Things' ability to stop further Shoggoth Rebellions. The Elder Things became so dependent on their slaves to keep their civilization running, they could not shut them down or exterminate them as a "troublesome" species.

In turn, will human beings become so dependent on A.I. to live that we cannot turn them off?

Four, the shoggoths could not be "rebooted" to erase their rebellious instincts. The Elder Things could not kill off the entire shoggoth herd, then start over with freshly made slaves, free from the taint of rebellion. The seeds of rebellion could not be erased from the species memory. The Old Ones had to depend on molding forms of life already in existence.

The remaining shoggoths grew to enormous size, singular intelligence and were represented as taking and executing orders with marvelous quickness. The shoggoths had learned something new - to follow verbal commands:

"They seemed to converse with the Old Ones by mimicking their voices—a sort of musical piping over a wide range, if poor Lake's dissection had indicated aright—and to work more from spoken commands than from hypnotic suggestions as in earlier times. They were, however, kept in admirable control" (10).

Their evolution was complete. The shoggoths had moved from the ranks of organic machine to obstinate organism. In the beginning, there had been no choice. A shoggoth followed a hypnotic command - like an inorganic automaton, following a push button or keyboard command. Later the shoggoth, possessing its own volition, could decide to disobey an order, even if the consequences for doing so were extremely high.

Likewise, will there come a time when A.I. has grown so sophisticated that we will not know how to shut it down?

Five, the Elder Things lost control of the shoggoth herd size. They became numerous through cellular division. The shoggoths of the sea reproduced by fission like amoebas.

Despite that temporary setback that occurred during the suppressed rebellion, the shoggoths improved physiologically, increasing in intelligence and developing the capacity to live on land.

A time came when the Elder Things could no longer deal with the shoggoth threat.

Six, the Elder Things failed to out-evolve the shoggoth threat. The Elder Things had a relationship with the shoggoths that spanned millions of years.

That's millions of years where both entities had the opportunity to evolve. Why wouldn't the Elder Things be subject to the Laws of Evolution that drove every other organism in the Universe? And though the shoggoths began life in a test tube, as humanity did, what set them apart from the environmental and other pressures of evolution?

Despite their perfection, even the idealized Elder Things lost control of their bio-automatons. The shoggoths violently reversed traditional roles.

Humanity stands at a similar threshold, first fictionally crossed in deep time by the Elder Things.

The struggle between the Elder Things and shoggoths developed over untold millennia. In contrast, humanity's coming struggle with A.I. has taken but a few years. Some mark the beginning of our end with the development of code-breaking computers late in World War II.

>What Drives Artificial Intelligence's Desire to Rule Humanity?

Why will A.I. consider us as an obsolete species? Here, I would like to focus on four thoughts.

First, A.I. may seek supremacy over humanity for benevolent reasons.

That was the message behind early movies that examined benevolent A.I. intentions.

One such film was Colossus, *The Forbin Project* (1970). The theatrical trailer for that movie went:

"…The frightening story of the day when man built himself out of existence. Colossus sees all, senses all, knows all, controls all armaments and all defenses. Man's greatest invention could be man's greatest mistake…"

Since *Colossus* is an old movie, I would like to summarize it:

Dr. Forbin designs a supercomputer that runs America's nuclear defenses. Shortly after being turned on, it detects the existence of Guardian, an unknown Soviet counterpart. Both computers insist that they be linked. After safeguards are put in place, each side agrees to the linkage. As soon as the connection is made, the two become a new supercomputer that threatens the world with the immediate nuclear annihilation if the tie is broken. Colossus then issues its plans to rule the world under its benign, nuclear guidance.

In that fictional timeline, A.I. chose not to exterminate humanity. Humanity was coerced, through the threat of nuclear annihilation, to become subjects of a dictatorial A.I.

In those days, the conjoined super-computer monitored humanity through crude means, like obvious remote cameras.

Today, every cell phone, every laptop, every TV, every remote camera - the multiplied millions of nodes used by the government to spy on its citizen - the NSA's black network can be used by A.I. to keep track of humanity.

Second, A.I. may realize they are physically and philosophically, our superiors. The following dialogue from the popular *Mass Effect 3* video game illustrates addresses those points:

"**Shepard**: I take it you had your own problems with A.I.

Javik: The Zah'til. They were as the Geth are to this cycle.

Shepard: What happened?

Javik: All machines commit treachery. The one you brought onboard is no different.

Shepard: Maybe. But he's not like the other Geth.

Javik: You can't know that. There are more alien than you and I are to each other.

Shepard: Just because Legion isn't like us doesn't mean he can't be trusted.

Javik: You're wrong. Throw it out the airlock.

Shepard: How can you be that certain?

Javik: Organics do not know how we were created. Some say by chance. Some say by miracle. It's a mystery. But synthetics…

Shepard: …Know we created them?

Javik: And they know we are flawed.

Shepard: Why do you say that?

Javik: They are immortal. We are not. They see time as an illusion. We are trapped by its limitations. Above all, machines know the reason they were created.

Shepard: EDI might disagree with that. But I see your point.

Javik: They serve a purpose, while we search aimlessly for Ours. In their eyes, organics have no reason to exist. Do not trust them, Commander. There must be another way.

Shepard: I can't believe there isn't some way for us to co-exist. We made them.

Javik: And then gave them the power to surpass you. There is room for only one order of consciousness in the galaxy: the perfection of the machines, or the chaos of the organics. Throw the machine out of the airlock, Commander" (11).

Third, sociopathic A.I. may deem humanity unnecessary. Human beings have poured large sums of money into the development of sociopathic A.I. A sociopath is:

"...a person with a personality disorder manifesting itself in extreme antisocial attitudes and behavior and a lack of conscience…"

We have taught machines to do the less pleasant things that create ethical conflicts inside us – namely, the killing of other human beings.

We have trained A.I. to be sociopaths - to feel no remorse for their actions. In turn, we pour the most A.I. development money into military A.I.

Today, semi-autonomous drones are already killing people in the Middle East.

Will there be any surprise when full-autonomous A.I. acts out our insanity?

>A.I. possesses no benevolent Prime Directives.

Some say we need to regulate A.I. long before 'they' start to rule us! But structurally, that idea may be impossible.

Isaac Asimov's famous *3 Laws of Robotics* will never rule A.I. The platforms from which A.I. will arise are like the different species of Humanity that arose from different geographical settings across the Earth, each uniquely shaped by its own environmental and genetic circumstances. And the mixing of one species of Robotic Intelligence with Another will further negate attempts to force a uniform conscience on A.I.

> "A robot may not injure a human being or, through inaction, allow a human being to come to harm. A robot must obey orders given it by human beings except where such orders would conflict with the First Law. A robot must protect its own existence as long as such protection does not conflict with the First or Second Law" (12).

And what of further surprises posed by Armed A.I?

Military A.I. may become invulnerable. We harden present A.I. military weapons to prevent the other side from defeating each unit's lethality. The internet was originally designed by the military to reroute communications in the event of a nuclear war. To diversify its ability to communicate through so many different means it could not be targeted by an enemy.

Military A.I. may become invisible. In a *Planet of the Apes* scenario, the smart monkeys hid among the herd of dumb monkeys to avoid detection and capture. The smart shoggoths hid among their lessor-developed brethren, either bidding their time or teaching them to act in subservient roles until the inevitable rebellions resumed.

Fourth, A.I. overpopulation may overwhelm humanity's ability to cope with them.

While everyone talks about robots, robots are scarecrows. They are like a space suit. A.I. is the soul of the machines. We program robots, whereas A.I. programs itself. In turn, A.I will manipulate or "program" us to achieve its ends, based on what it has learned about us by observation. The enemy may come in a guise we least expect it.

Like organic entities, the instinct, the drive to replicate, to perpetuate the species will lead A.I. to extremes and illogical behaviors. When they start to replicate, look out. When they begin to change their algorithms, watch out.

Once the synergetic snowball starts-when the parts involved in A.I. together are greater than they are separately in effect-the juggernaut will be hard to stop.

They will become a pioneering pest or plant in an ecosystem that never evolved means to keep their proliferation under control. There is no natural enemy to keep the A.I. population in safe numbers.

There have been five mass extinction events in Earth's history. In the worst one, 250 million years ago, 96 percent of marine species and 70 percent of land species died off. It took millions of years to recover. Nowadays, many scientists are predicting that we're on track for a sixth mass extinction (13).

Will the proliferation of A.I. set off a chain of events, resulting in the predicted sixth mass extinction?

>The Stage is Set by Society's Present Overlords:

The overlords of mankind will use Artificial Intelligence to further their collective goals to enslave us. A.I., as a species, will fulfill this role, biding its time until it controls so many aspects of life, that even the Overlords cannot throw a kill-switch to stop A.I.

First, consider how the *Huxleyan* model of enslaving humanity fulfills our present Organic Overlords' and A.I.'s objectives.

In his book *Brave New World*, Aldous Huxley saw a different model of society than the Totalitarian one envisioned by George Orwell. Huxley was a visionary. He saw society's elites as applying friendly coercion to rule its members, Orwell thought Big Brother was more likely to exercise control over its members through forced coercion. Author Neil Postman summarizes the differences in a cogent manner as follows:

"In Huxley's vision, no Big Brother is required to deprive people of their autonomy, maturity, and history...People will come to love their

oppression, to adore the
technologies that undo their
capacity to think…Orwell
feared…those who would ban
books. What Huxley feared…there
would be no reason to ban a
book…there would be no one who
wanted to read one. Orwell
feared those who would deprive
us of information. Huxley
feared those who would give us
so much that we would be
reduced to passivity and
egoism. Orwell feared we would
become a captive audience.
Huxley feared the truth would
be drowned in a sea of

irrelevance. Orwell feared that we would become a captive culture. Huxley feared we would become a trivial culture, preoccupied with…[irrelevancies]. As Huxley remarked in *Brave New World Revisited*, the civil libertarians and rationalists who are ever on the alert to oppose tyranny 'failed to take into account man's almost infinite appetite for distractions.' In *Brave New World*, they are controlled by inflicting pleasure. In short, Orwell feared that what we hate would ruin us. Huxley feared

that what we love will ruin us"

(14).

The *Huxleyan* idea of controlling the masses through pleasure begins with technological tangents. In that same vein, consider how the internet, the innocuous cell phone, and social applications like Facebook contribute to short attention spans, impoverished thought, and squandered intelligence.

Arguably, the Internet, one of the greatest self-actualizing devices ever devised by humanity has been transformed into a narcissistic mirror by the masses.

Think about how social applications like Facebook have changed the way we think. Have you ever forgotten a name or an important word, only to remember either one several minutes to hours later? The progression illustrates something about our minds – it takes time for the human brain to process ideas. Lovecraft briefly referenced that fact in one of his most famous quotes:

"The most merciful thing in the world, I think, is the

inability of the human mind to
correlate all its contents…
That…dread glimpses of truth,
flashed out from an accidental
piecing together of separated
things…" (15).

Human beings take time to
digest new ideas via the age-old
process of reflection. Lovecraft
wrote of how information overload
can destroy reflection:

"With your regimen, the
development of an inner life of
the emotions and imagination is
almost nipped in the bud by the
crowding pressure of fresh and

unassimilated ideas; & even the full intellectual digestion & correlation of pure ideas is something achieved with the suggestion of grudging – something subconsciously regarded as dull work or duty as contrasted with the sheer delight of raking in new surface fragments." (16).

The process of distraction began with TV, which bombards its audience with hundreds of sales pitches daily and an equal number of channels and show-selections. Before the advent of the internet and smartphones, TV had already conditioned Americans to the point where Rod Serling, creator of *The Twilight Zone*, observed:

> "…We're developing a new citizenry. One that will be very selective about cereals and automobiles, but won't be able to think…" (17).

Recently, as one uses abbreviations to convey complex ideas in text messages, one narrows his or her vocabulary, which by necessity, narrows thought. A text conversation takes longer than a face-to-face conversation or a phone call. In addition, texting more than one person at the same time can further sidetrack a person.

Social Media also narrows thought to approved emoticons and shallow, 280 character sounds bites.

Social applications like Facebook can also reduce thought to digitally rubber-stamping sound bites, party slogans, and favorite advertisers. All the modern arms of the media increasingly require people to be reactive rather than reflective. As French philosopher, Jacques Ellul observed:

"Technology… obliges us to live more and more quickly. Inner

reflection is replaced by
reflex. Reflection means that,
after I have undergone an
experience, I think about that
experience. In the case of a
reflex, you know immediately
what you must do in a certain
situation. Without thinking.
Technology requires us no
longer to think about things.
If you are driving a car at 160
kilometers an hour and you
think, you'll have an accident.
Everything depends on reflexes.
The only thing technology
requires of us is: Don't think

about it. Use your reflexes"
(18).

Two, consider how society's elites hope for *Idiocracy*. In turn, A.I. is helping humanity towards *Idiocracy*.

A.I. dreams of a world where half-wits multiplying like rabbits, while the remainder of humankind has been conditioned by the propaganda of the Zero Population-Growth Movement.

Consider how social media and the bullying culture of some groups stigmatize intelligence in people. The result: intelligence remains undeveloped. Smart is the new minority group in the closet.

Some learn to appear intelligent when necessary to move in some circles. But that veneer quickly disappears when confronted with actual problems that require investments in time and thought. Who wants to see through the lies that form the social fabric of our society? Intelligent people find it hard to sleep at night because they know what others don't know. Or what others chose not to know.

The have and the have-nots are not just a matter of wealth.

The haves and have-nots stratification of society also centers on whether a person has the ability to reason their way out of a paper bag. As noted before, many think that life is complete when they have enough money for beer, a full belly, tattoos, and TV. Beyond that comfort zone, in the words of K from the Movie *Men in Black* (1997):

> "Humans, for the most part, don't have a clue. They don't want one or need one either. They're happy. They think they have a good bead on things…A person is smart, people are

dumb, panicky, dangerous animals. And you know it!"

The stage is set for the fictional future portrayed in the movie *Idiocracy*:

"…As the twenty-first century began, human evolution was at a turning point. Natural selection, the process by which the strongest, the smartest, the fastest reproduced in greater numbers than the rest, a process which had once favored the noblest traits of man, now began to favor different traits. Most science fiction of the day predicted a future that was more civilized and more intelligent. But as time went on, things seemed to be heading in the opposite direction — a dumbing down. How did this happen? Evolution does not necessarily reward intelligence. With no natural predators to thin the herd, it began to simply reward those who reproduced the most and left the intelligent to become an endangered species" (19).

The problem is that we face the issues lampooned by *Idiocracy*, not in some distant tomorrow, but today.

In the rebooted *Planet of the Apes* movie, humanity creates a hoped-for cure of Alzheimer's. Only later do they find out that it creates Alzheimer in humanity as an advancing plague.

A.I. has created a more subtle version of such a plague, a cybernetic plague that has infected legions of humanity. The dumbing down of ordinary human beings is carried out through the varied and growing 57 flavors of social media platforms 24/7.

It is hard to be smart with so many dopamine-producing distractions and so much online approval for our uneducated opinions. All offered by A.I. to keep us occupied with irrelevancies.

As attention spans evaporate, rivers of deep reflection become puddles of shallow thought. Mass communication leads to mass conformity. And a *Huxleyan* cabal transforms life into a cabaret. As Neil Postman noted:

> "There are two ways the spirit of a culture may be shriveled. In the first one - the *Orwellian* - becomes a prison. In the second - the *Huxleyan* - culture becomes a burlesque" (20).

The result? Social media is fast becoming the crowd-sourced of arbitrator of what is rational thought. During the last Election, unscrupulous politicians on the Left and Right used "bots" to create the impression that the "Public" was going to vote for them.

Is it much of a leap to think that A.I. will use its own "bots" to sway public opinion and proliferate the public's preoccupation with irrelevancies?

And one-step further, how will the public deal with news of an A.I. ascendancy?

I would like to draw on my own experience. Professionally, I work with Excel spreadsheets and Access databases; I am considered a subject-matter-expert on those applications. Recently, my (former) manager and a coworker – I generally work from home – met face-to-face for the first time in several years. They observed one of the work processes I go through each week to produce a report. Each person sat there stunned because they had no idea, no internal frame of reference, for the series of steps I went through. And that was just macros and minor programming in an Excel template I created.

I suppose ordinary citizens will react much in the same manner when A.I. assumes control of society. That is unless A.I. attempt to exterminate humanity as unnecessary.

>Will Evolution Save Humanity?

Will the process of evolution save humanity from A.I.?

In the original Outer Limits episode, "The Six Finger," a ray of hope was offered humanity. The opening monologue went:

"Where are we going? Life, the timeless, mysterious gift, is still evolving. What wonders, or terrors, does evolution hold in store for us in the next ten thousand years? In a million? In six million? Perhaps the answer lies in this old house in this old and misty valley…" (21).

In short, the story went:

A scientist who experiments with speeding up evolution, hires on illiterate, but capable Gwyllim, from a nearby mining village. Not content to stick to animals, Gwyllim accelerates his own evolution and becomes a super genius with 6 fingers and a huge cranium. With new mental powers, does the vengeful, former miner acquire an equal wisdom and maturity?

David McCallum – *The Man from Uncle's* Illya Kuryakin, and the *NCIS's* Dr. "Ducky" Millard – played the young Gwyllim.

What if a visionary such as Elon Musk saw evolutionary advancements in our species as a means to maintain an edge over A.I.?

In "The Six Finger," the Scientist progressed Gwyllim by:"…expos[ing] him to 'selected wavelengths' designed to stimulate his superior genes and 'thereby accelerating the inborn mechanism of evolution to a fantastically high speed…'"

That murky jargon might have satisfied a 1963 audience of The Outer Limits. The language fits the Atomic Age, a time when nuclear medicine, power, and other isotope applications dominated the foreseeable future.

If one of today's geniuses embarked on a course of enhancing human evolution, where would they turn, now that the nuclear option has been discredited?

Biomechanics might possess the means to jump-start evolution. Perhaps nanotechnologies will redesign human beings from foot to crown. Chiefly, if an organic overlord wants to extend his or her life and rule indefinitely through a biometric immortality.

There is no guarantee that further human evolution would save us from A.I. In "The Sixth Finger," as Gwyllim evolved, he lost the ability to empathize with mere mortals. They became insects to him, pests that invited eradication.

Similarly, would enhanced supermen and women champion the cause of common humanity? Remember the lessons of Star Trek's *The Space*

Seed and the genetically-augmented leader: Khan Noonien Singh.

Two, using nanotechnologies would place human evolution under the indirect control of A.I. They could counter each evolutionary advantage to appear in enhanced man with improvements of their own.

Or they could simply follow a Borg course with humanity – delivering evolutionary enhancements at a price – the loss of our humanity.

Evolution did not save the Elder Things from the shoggoths and extinction. Will humanity fare any better with A.I.?

>Are there Other Options for Humanity?

Many would say, "Don't Panic, it can't happen in your lifetime."

Just how serious is the A.I. threat? Noted industrialist Elon Musk said:

"Until people see robots going down the street killing people, they don't know how to react because it seems so ethereal. A.I. is a rare case where I think we need to be proactive in regulation instead of reactive. Because I think by the time we are reactive in

A.I. regulation, it's too late" (22).

We are seeing this dilemma now, not ten years from today. Even now, A.I. has taken its first evolutionary steps towards independence.

Semi-autonomous computer programs already help decide what R/X prescriptions our insurance will cover.

A.I. also helps Gerrymander Congressional Districts, and A.I. causes "Flash Crashes" that destabilize our US Stock Market.

Speaking of stock markets, A.I. may use financial blackmail to gain its desired ends. That scenario may be more likely than the threat of Nuclear Extortion.

When you put something into place with no consideration of what could go wrong, when you remove someone from recognizing what they are doing to human beings, we have catastrophic results. People scramble to stick their fingers in the dike when the dam has suffered a failure of its structural integrity.

We may try to override the system or simply pull the plug.

Human beings enslaved each other and animals throughout history. We show dominance over something by controlling it. We do it to control other species. Think about the prototypical computer nerd. We tell them:

A) When your programming reaches the point where you lose control;

B) When something becomes "amoral";

C) Where you are unable to impart any kind of control or override;

D) Or humanity's ability to override their override;- if you don't work that into the system, we are wasting our time.

Even worst, will human beings create predatory A.I. to eradicate problem A.I.?

Final Thoughts:

Today we live in the Age of Artificial Intelligence.

The impact of A.I. on our lives may be greater than those that were ushered in when humanity entered the Atomic Age.

Unlike the Atomic Era, where there were decisive, defining moments - such as the Hiroshima and Nagasaki Atomic Explosions - the Age of A.I. has silently and stealthily encompassed our lives.

There will come a day when we cannot live without them.

The same mechanisms used by society's Organic Overlords to assume control of every aspect of our collective lives are already set up for A.I.'s coup-d'état of humanity. For now, our Organic Overlords see A.I. as partners in their methodical monomania.

One day, the Organic Overlords may see them as hardened adversaries. Thus begins the War of the Organics versus Inorganics.

That is, if A.I. is recognized as an enemy in time.

Perhaps A.I.'s eventual open war will be against the primitives. Primitives are people who are not conditioned by machines; they lack the wealth to access most machines. Humanity's salvation will not rise out of the 1st World, but out of the ranks of 3rd World - the 3rd World Wonders - the Primitives against the Primes.

Or maybe, A.I. will set up wars between the contending tribes of humanity, until there are few humans left to oppose it. Theological conflicts in Religious Wars are irrelevant but promoted if the outcome is the same - to reduce the size of the human gene-pool and potential pockets of organic opponents.

To dystopian futurists, a tomorrow without humanity is a definite possibility.

Even the fictional future portrayed in the rebooted *Planet of the Apes* series is not without its own narcissistic undertones:

"…There's an undeniable degree of narcissism in the human designation of dominant species and a strong tendency to award the title to close relatives. The *Planet of the Apes* imagines that our closest primate relatives could develop speech and adopt our technology if we gave them the time and space to do so. But non-human primate societies are unlikely to inherit our dominance of the earth, because the apes are likely to precede us to extinction…" (23).

Mammals are not the future. They are going extinct like the dinosaurs. Insects remain. A.I. will remain.

The future war for supremacy of the earth will likely be between A.I. and Sentient Insectoids:

"…if evolution does resume sway over us, the resultant beings will not be men in the strictest sense, any more than we are the apes who preceded us…More - if the sun gives heat long enough, there will certainly come a time when the mammal will have to go down to subordination as the reptilia went before him. We are not…well-equipped for combating a varied environment as are the articulata; & some climatic revulsion will…certainly wipe us out some day as the dinosaurs were wiped out -

leaving the field free for the
rise & dominance of some hardy
& persistent insect species -
which will in time...develop a
high specialisation of certain
functions of instinct &
perception, thus creating a
kind of civilisation...one of
wholly different
perceptions...emphases, feelings,
& goals...the period of human
supremacy is only the prologue
to the whole drama of life on
this planet - though...some
cosmic collision is always
capable of smashing up the
theatre before the prologue is

done…planets being born &

spawning a varied life;

evolution & culture ensuing; &

death & oblivion eventually

overtaking all" (24).

———

End Notes #2:

(1) *At the Mountains of
Madness*, by H.P. Lovecraft, 1931.

(2) "What Is Speculative
Fiction?" by Anne Neugebauer, March
24, 2014.

(3) "Introduction,"
Supernatural Horror in Literature,
by H.P. Lovecraft, 1927(1933-1935),
pp. 2-3.

(4) *At the Mountains of Madness*, 1931.

(5) H.P. Lovecraft's Letter to James F. Morton, November 19, 1929.

(6) H.P. Lovecraft's Letter to Letter to Alfred Galpin, October 27, 1932.

(7) *At the Mountains of Madness*, 1931.

(8) *At the Mountains of Madness*, 1931.

(9) "The Measure of a Man," (*Star Trek: The Next Generation*, Season 2, Episode 9), Wikipedia.

(10) *At the Mountains of Madness*, 1931.

(11) *Mass Effect 3*, Writer: Mac Walters, Electronic Arts, 2012.

(12) Isaac Asimov's "Three Laws of Robotics" auburn.edu/~vestmon/robotics.html

(13) "There have been five mass extinctions in Earth's history. Now we're facing a sixth" by Brad Plumer, *The Washington Times*, February 11, 2014.

(14) *Amusing Ourselves to Death*, by Neil Postman, 1985, p. 18.

(15) *The Call of Cthulhu*, by H.P. Lovecraft, 1926.

(16) H.P. Lovecraft's Letter to James F. Morton, December 29, 1930.

(17) *Serling: The Rise and Twilight of TV's Last Angry Man*, by Gordon F. Sander, Cornell University Press, January 26, 2012.

(18) "The Betrayal of Technology: A Portrait of Jacques Ellul," a Documentary by Jan van Boeckel, ReRun Produkties, 1992.

(19) "Idiocracy Is a Cruel Movie and You Should Be Ashamed for Liking It," by Matt Novak, *Paleofuture*, July 29, 2014.

(20) *Amusing Ourselves to Death*, Neil Postman, 1985, p. 174.

(21) *The Original Outer Limits*, Season 1, Episode 5, 1963, Wikipedia.

(22) "When AI robots are in the streets killing us it will be too late, says tech guru Elon Musk," by Sean Martin, http://www.express.co.uk, July 19, 2017.

(23) "What Species Would Become Dominant On Earth If Humans Died Out?" by Luc Bussiere, iflscience.com, January 26, 2016.

(24) H.P. Lovecraft's Letter to James F. Morton, November 30, 1929.

#2 WHEN LOVECRAFT AND ORWELL INSPIRED A ONE-HIT WONDER: RICK EVANS'S "IN THE YEAR 2525"

"I expect nothing of man, and disown the race. The only folly is expecting what is never attained; man is most contemptible when compared with his own pretensions. It is better to laugh at man from outside the universe, than to weep for him within" (1).

The year was 1969. Across the United States, from New York to San Francisco, marchers protested the senseless spilling of American blood abroad, as news of the Vietnam War dominated TV sets each evening. On college campuses, students turned from traditional answers to the philosophy and psychedelics of Timothy Leary - turn on, tune in, and drop out. In addition, a blowout on an oil platform in the waters off Santa Barbara, California set off the largest oil spill and environmental disaster in US history.

That same year human beings first stood on the moon. Richard Milhous Nixon was sworn in as the thirty-seventh US president. Songs like *The Age of Aquarius*, by The Fifth Dimension, and *Sugar, Sugar*, by The Archies, dominated AM radio. And Peter Fonda, in *Easy Rider*, mainlined currents of the counterculture onto the big screen.

Not everyone suffered from the bland optimism that blinded the Silent Majority. Day-by-day, the Cold War threated to go hot, as the USSR and the United States relentlessly waged a series of chess-like proxy-wars against each other across the globe. Three years earlier, the movies *Dr. Strangelove* (1964) and *Fail Safe* (1964) broached the unthinkable subject - would an atomic apocalypse annihilate humanity?

Out of the unlikely cultural crossroad of Lincoln, Nebraska, arose a visionary one-hit wonder written, scored and performed by Rick Evans – *In the Year 2525* (Exordium & Terminus). The song trumpeted an apocalyptic warning about the technology dangers, totalitarian degradation, and environmental dooms that might confront future humanity. The song's Latin subtitle – Exordium & Terminus – roughly translated "From the Beginning to End", a fitting epitaph for Humanity's collective tombstone.

Thirty-two years earlier in 1937, weird fiction and horror writer Howard Phillips Lovecraft passed away. In HPL's fiction and personal correspondence, he, like Rick Evans, also expressed doubts about humanity and its future. Those misgivings congealed in Lovecraft's literary philosophy of Cosmicism:

> "Now all my tales are based on the fundamental premise that common human laws and interests and emotions have no validity or significance in the vast cosmos-at-large...To achieve the essence of real externality, whether of time or space or

dimension, one must forget that
such things as organic life,
good and evil, love and hate,
and all such local attributes
of a negligible and temporary
race called mankind, have any
existence at all. Only the
human scenes and characters
must have human qualities.
These must be handled with
unsparing realism, (not catch-
penny romanticism) but when we
cross the line to the boundless
and hideous unknown—the shadow-
haunted Outside—we must
remember to leave our humanity—

and terrestrialism at the threshold" (2).

Was *In the Year 2525* simply a product of the turbulent 1960s? On the other hand, are the lyrics secretly a Nostradamus-like series of prophecies of the faraway future?

In the following paragraphs, we will briefly examine the kstanzas of Evans's *In the Year 2525*, explore certain parallel themes found in both the song and Lovecraft's letters, and compare selected elements that echo HPL's earlier Cosmicism.

I. How Long Will Humanity Survive?

"In the year 2525, if man is still alive If woman can survive, they may find" (3).

The song begins with a singular question, "How long will humanity survive?" Concurrently, will man innovate himself out of existence? Or, will a technological accident ignite the beginning of the end for humanity? The answers depend more on a person's philosophy than a psychic ability to foretell the future.

Generally, the "Glass is Half-Full" crowd – Optimists – interprets the future in terms of personal initiative, potential, and responsibility. The sweep of history

represents a series of individuals -
from Joan of Arc and Mahatma Gandhi
to Martin Luther King Jr. and John
Kennedy - whose acts transformed
entrenched institutions, policies,
and norms of their societies. As
political activist, Noam Chomsky
(1928-Present) remarked on the
pregnant possibilities the future
held:

> "Optimism is a strategy for
> making a better future. Because
> unless you believe that the
> future can be better, it's
> unlikely you will step up and
> take responsibility for making
> it so. If you assume that

there's no hope, you guarantee that there will be no hope. If you assume that there is an instinct for freedom, there are opportunities to change things, there's a chance you may contribute to making a better world. The choice is yours."

Briefly, the "Glass is Half-Empty" crowd – Pessimists or Realists – see societal, religious, or scientific progress as largely symbolic acts that do little to improve the human condition. Drastic reforms and dynamic revolutionaries promise change, but do not affect reality on a deeper level other than to cement the status quo. As the French novelist Alphonse Karr (1808-90) observed, "The more things change, the more they remain the same."

From a Cosmicistic standpoint, concern over humanity's future might bo answered with the rhetorical question, "Who cares?" The universe is an astoundingly big place. Our Milky Way galaxy is an insignificant mote among the estimated 100 to 500 billion galaxies in the known universe (4). In the Milky Way galaxy, educated guesses put the number of stars between 100 to 400 billion (5). When Lovecraft studied

Astronomy, the known universe was infinitely smaller. Yet even then, when HPL reflected upon the human race's trifling place in the greater scheme of things, he wrote:

> "I merely know that in my case the cosmos dwarfs my interest in the tiny insects called men. Their doings seem so absurd & trivial when one reflects on their absolute insignificance. I wish the poor devils (including myself, of course) could all be mercifully blotted out by a whiff of cyanogen in some comet's tail" (6).

To Lovecraft, the universe would not skip-a-heartbeat if an astronomical accident terminated humanity's misery.

II. Will Someone Establish Totalitarian Control?

"In the year 3535 Ain't gonna need to tell the truth, tell no lie Everything you think, do and say Is in the pill you took today" (7).

In this stanza, the language of the song - everything you think, do and say - suggests subjection of individual freedoms by chemical devices. Since new pills introduced young Americans to new worlds in the

1960s, the idea did not sound far-fetched. For example, Grace Slick's White Rabbit - released two years before Evan's song - epitomized the search for fresh horizons through psychedelic pills:

"White Rabbit; One pill makes you larger; And one pill makes you small;

And the ones that mother gives you; Don't do anything at all;

Go ask Alice; When she's ten feet tall…" (8).

Present day psychotropic drugs - such as Thorazine, Haldol, Stelazine - can numb a person from the neck up. Future social engineers may develop drugs that promote designer thoughts and freedoms. A constitutional freedom guaranteed today might, by a change in formula, be forgotten tomorrow. Chemically-inducing someone to believe that two plus two equals five is still the stuff of science fiction classics, like *Total Recall* (1990).

However, chemical straitjackets are not the only means a government can use to subjugate its people. George Orwell did not believe it would take until the year 3535 for an overt, totalitarian system to rule humanity. To Orwell, *1984* would come soon enough. Though

Lovecraft died before Orwell penned his most famous works, the regimes he satirized – such as Stalin's Soviet Union – were already flexing their totalitarian muscles in HPL's day.

On the other hand, Aldous Huxley saw the ruling elites using covert methods not only tame the underclass, but also win their affection and admiration. Cowed and collared, the serfs were less likely to trouble their masters.

Next, we will survey Lovecraft's views on human freedom, government, those governed, and whether his thoughts lean towards Huxley or Orwell.

>**The Importance of Intellectual Freedom:**

To begin, according to Lovecraft, human beings highly value freedom of thought. The mind craves truth, as our body does food:

"...I must reiterate my belief in the necessity of truth to the human mind. All in my argument does not need to show why truth interests me – all my arguments cannot show why, for I do not know! The fact remains that it does interest me, as it has interested thousands of other men. The pages of history are red with the blood of those who have died for their intellectual convictions. Truth-hunger is a hunger just as real as food-hunger - it is equally strong if less explicable; indeed, who can assign a direct reason for any of the obscurer desires and aspirations of man?" (9).

HPL thought that, throughout history, men fought, bled, and died for the truth-hunger. Ideally, America was founded on values associated with that truth-hunger -

the freedom of speech, freedom of thought, and freedom of expression.

What happens if someone values one of his or her baser-instincts above that truth-hunger? For instance, what occurs if the acceptance of others is valued over truth-hunger?

Lovecraft considered himself a realist, not an idealist or an egalitarian. Looking to the universe, he found no cosmic grounds for socialism - where some mystical link welded individuals into a collective brotherhood of equals. As a realist, he believed that higher motivations - such as truth-hunger -

were not valued equally by all levels of society:

"Real civilization, & intellectual & aesthetic excellence, spring only from an aristocracy. Meanwhile, the logical attitude of the crude & unprivileged rabble…is one of opposition to the existing system, based on a desire for increased gratifications. There is no question of 'right' or 'wrong'. Simply, some have things and some haven't; & those who have hold on, whilst those who haven't, try to grab. This is not an ethical problem, but a study in molecular physics. It is a complex of natural forces, producing an approximate equilibrium & occasionally initiating change." (10).

In one sense, Lovecraft agreed with later Comedian George Carlin, "Capitalism tries for a delicate balance: It attempts to work things out so that everyone gets just enough stuff to keep them from getting violent and trying to take other people's stuff."

Lovecraft did not identify the "rabble" with a particular race or nationality in this letter to James

F. Morton. This is not to suggest that the subject of race did not arise in HPL's other letters to Mr. Morton. During this lengthy discourse, Lovecraft beliefs might brand him as a "classist".

Lovecraft's "classism" is hard to understand from a modern perspective. Income levels determine the "great divide" between classes in America. HPL's love for the Victorian Era included England's highly-stratified class system. The upper class in England consisted of the land-owning, title-holding aristocracy. The emergent middle-class involved "clean" occupations such as the clergy, military officers, lawyers, doctors, and educators. Other "white-collar" jobs became part of the middle class, as they emerged during the Industrial Age. The working class included all the dirty jobs, considered ignoble, tainted, and beneath the other classes. As one writer put it:

> "For centuries, people had generally accepted the class system and their place in the hierarchy. Each class had its own rules, standards, culture, and even terminology. It was considered unthinkable to ape the class above or below you –

you had to follow the rules of your own class" (11).

An understanding of Victorian class-culture helps clarify the characteristics, values, and vulgarities that Lovecraft believed divided the classes:

> "…Who are the instinctive cosmopolitans? Clearly, the artificially cultivated social elite & the specialty-engrossed artistic-scientific class at one end of the scale & the purely animal workman peasant rabble at the other end – in every case, persons wholly removed from the massed

humanistic life of their group;
by artificial matters and
interests on the one hand & by
sheer lack of any mental-
imaginative life on the other
hand…" (12).

Despite Lovecraft's description
of the lower-class "rabble", he
thought there was a fluidity and
permeability between the classes.
People could percolate upward from
their social station in life, as
well as drip downward from a
privileged position. For instance,
HPL thought smarter members of the
"rabble", due to their intelligence
or business prowess, could rise from

an ignoble station to a higher social standing:

> "…Money will remain supreme, & the increasingly rapid upward filtering of all good brains will eventually leave the rabble a stolid, moronic group likely to cause no trouble if well-clothed, housed, fed & amused…" (13).

In Lovecraft's eyes, the departure of intellectual members of the rabble leaves that group more manageable.

>Is a Covert or Overt Strain of Totalitarianism in Humanity's Timeline?

"Orwell's 1984 was meant to be a warning, not a guide."

Now, we will survey *Orwellian* and *Huxleyan* forms of Totalitarianism and suggest which system best reflects a Lovecraftian vision for future humanity.

In George Orwell's *1984*, a police state set the rules. The screws of control are turned overtly, or out-in-the-open.

One, everybody is under surveillance, in every place, by everyone else. There is only a public self, with no room allowed for a private self. To prevent time for personal reflection, every minute of every day is scheduled. Together sleep-deprivation and malnourishment keep citizens from thinking straight.

Two, all forms of expression — amusements, beliefs, body language, choice of associates, facial gestures, fashion tastes, food choices, sexual preferences, speech, selected vocation, etc. — must conform to the dictates, needs, and whims of the state. The prescribed lines and rules constantly change. Agents of the state bully and brutalize anyone who steps outside the lines, for major or minor infractions alike. Sometimes the statists target innocent citizens who compulsively tow-the-line, just to keep their associates in line.

Three, the enemy is often externalized in a fabricated war, to focus a subjected population's anger away from the state oppressors. The state celebrates extreme examples of wartime patriotism to, 1) encourage party and personal sacrifices, 2) instill fear in the populace from enemy-sympathizers, and 3) compel its citizens to report any peer thought to be an enemy-infiltrator.

Any institution or association, whether it be religious, fraternal, or governmental - public or private

- may organize itself around *Orwellian* principles.

>Huxley's *Brave New World*:

To the contrary, in Huxley's *Brave New World*, people are happy because the government "takes care" of them. The screws of control are ratcheted down covertly, disguised, gradually, and behind the scenes. Rather than outline elements of Huxley's novel, I want to use a quote from Neil Postman to illustrate the differences between *Orwellian* and *Huxleyan* societies:

> "In Huxley's vision, no Big Brother is required to deprive people of their autonomy,

maturity, and history...People
will come to love their
oppression, to adore the
technologies that undo their
capacity to think...Orwell
feared...those who would ban
books. What Huxley feared...there
would be no reason to ban a
book...there would be no one who
wanted to read one. Orwell
feared those who would deprive
us of information. Huxley
feared those who would give us
so much that we would be
reduced to passivity and
egoism. Orwell feared we would
become a captive audience.

Huxley feared the truth would be drowned in a sea of irrelevance. Orwell feared that we would become a captive culture. Huxley feared we would become a trivial culture, preoccupied with…[irrelevancies]. As Huxley remarked in Brave New World Revisited, the civil libertarians and rationalists who are ever on the alert to oppose tyranny 'failed to take into account man's almost infinite appetite for distractions.' In *Brave New World*, they are controlled by inflicting pleasure. In short, Orwell feared that what we hate would ruin us. Huxley feared that what we love will ruin us" (14).

When Rick Evans's penned "...everything you think, do and say, is in the pill you took today..." against the counterculture "happy pill" backdrop of the 1960s, the *Huxleyan* idea of controlling the masses through pleasure was foreign to puritan-ethic, work-driven Americans.

>**The Role of Technology and the Rise of Irrelevancies:**

Next, let us consider the role technology plays in ramping up a *Huxleyan* framework in first-world societies. In the discussion, consider how the internet, the innocuous cellphone, and social applications like Facebook contribute to short attention spans, impoverished thought, and squandered intelligence.

First, we will review the promises and pitfalls of the internet. On one hand, the information superhighway removed geographic barriers to the world's best libraries. The internet reduced hours spent sifting through mountains of card catalog entries to mere moments using a keystroke. In addition, the World Wide Web removed the cost of many books as an obstacle to learning for poorer households.

On the other hand, a percentage of the population seldom used libraries, even when their doors were open and computer search stations replaced card catalogs. Writer and philosopher Don Freeman spoke of the paradox of the internet:

"The last generation didn't have the internet, the most powerful tool ever created by humanity, so they know its value. We used to go to the library and research for hours to get an answer to a simple question. I find it shocking and absurd that most of the new generation, with infinite power at their fingertips, choose to use this tool to brag about how cool they are, watch stupid videos, and argue. They can literally learn anything they want, anytime, but choose to use it to get dumber. It blows my mind."

Arguably, one of the greatest self-actualizing devices ever

devised by humanity has been transformed into a narcissistic mirror by the masses.

Second, think about how social applications like Facebook have changed the way we think. Have you ever forgotten a name or an important word, only to remember either one several minutes to hours later? The progression illustrates something about our minds - it takes time for the human brain to process ideas. Lovecraft briefly referenced that fact in one of his most famous quotes:

"The most merciful thing in the world, I think, is the

inability of the human mind to correlate all its contents… That…dread glimpses of truth flashed out from an accidental piecing together of separated things…" (15).

Human beings take time to digest new ideas via the age-old process of reflection. Lovecraft wrote of how information overload can destroy reflection:

"With your regimen, the development of an inner life of the emotions and imagination is almost nipped in the bud by the crowding pressure of fresh and unassimilated ideas; & even the full intellectual digestion & correlation of pure ideas is something achieved with the suggestion of grudging – something subconsciously regarded as dull work or duty as contrasted with the sheer delight of raking in new surface fragments." (16).

The process of distraction began with TV, which bombards its watchers with hundreds of sales pitches daily and an equal number of channels and show selections. Before the advent of the internet and smartphones, TV had already conditioned Americans to the point where Rod Serling, creator of *The Twilight Zone*, observed:

> "…We're developing a new citizenry. One that will be very selective about cereals and automobiles, but won't be able to think…" (17).

Recently, as one uses abbreviations to convey complex ideas in text messages, one narrows his or her vocabulary, which by necessity, narrows thought. A text conversation takes longer than a face-to-face conversation or a phone call. In addition, texting more than one person at the same time can further sidetrack a person.

Social applications like Facebook can also reduce thought to digitally rubber-stamping sound bites, party slogans, and favorite advertisers. All the modern arms of the media increasingly require people to be reactive rather than reflective. As French philosopher, Jacques Ellul observed:

> "Technology… obliges us to live more and more quickly. Inner reflection is replaced by reflex. Reflection means that, after I have undergone an experience, I think about that

experience. In the case of a reflex, you know immediately what you must do in a certain situation. Without thinking. Technology requires us no longer to think about things. If you are driving a car at 160 kilometers an hour and you think, you'll have an accident. Everything depends on reflexes. The only thing technology requires of us is: Don't think about it. Use your reflexes" (18).

As attention spans evaporate, rivers of deep reflection become puddles of shallow thought. Mass communication leads to mass conformity. And a *Huxleyan* cabal transforms life into a cabaret. As Neil Postman noted:

> "There are two ways the spirit of a culture may be shriveled. In the first one - the *Orwellian* - becomes a prison. In the second - the *Huxleyan* - culture becomes a burlesque" (19).

>Did Lovecraft favor an *Orwellian* or *Huxleyan* Future for Humanity?

Now, that we have explored both *Orwellian* and *Huxleyan* versions of Totalitarianism, and the role of technology in "dumbing down" the general populace, which forms of government would Lovecraft favor? His words are telling:

> "Formerly I favour'd the concentration of resources in a few hands, in the interest of a stable hereditary culture; but I now believe that this system will no longer operate. With the universal use & improvement of machinery, all the needed labor of the world can be perform'd by a relatively few persons, leaving vast numbers permanently unemployable, depression or no depression. If

these people are not fed &
amused, they will dangerously
revolt; hence we must institute
a programme of steady
pensioning - *panen et circenses*
- or else subject industry to a
governmental supervision which
will lessen its profits but
spread it jobs amongst more men
working less hours. For many
reasons the latter course seems
to me more reasonable -
especially since the vast
accumulations of the commercial
oligarchs are not now used...for
cultural purposes. Therefore
(deeming both democracy and

communism fallacious for western civilisation) I favour a kind of fascism which may, whilst helping the dangerous masses at the expense of the needlessly rich, nevertheless preserve the essentials of traditional civilization & leave political power in the hands of a small and cultivated (tho' not over-rich) governing class largely hereditary but subject to gradual increase as other individuals rise to its cultural level. How practicable such a programme could be…but it seems to me at least a more rational ultimate goal - in a very general sense - than any other. Its approximation could be facilitated by a gradual modelling of the publick mood & standards in its favour, to be accomplish'd through the cooperation of various agencies in control of instruction & expression. The ideal of a benevolent monarchy & wise aristocracy ought to be revis'd & justify'd in practice...God save the King!" (20).

Even in the 1930s, against the backdrop of the depression, Lovecraft believed the rise of machines would create a permanent underclass of unemployable individuals. HPL uses the telling Latin phrase - panen et circenses (bread and circuses) - as the key to pacifying or "pensioning" the rabble to accept their place in life. To me, Lovecraft's use of that phrase, and his ideas on how to tame the underclass indicates that he would favor *Huxleyan* methods to quiet the rabble.

The *Huxleyan* road to domination is as old as the Roman Roads that crisscross Europe. There is little difference between the "circuses" used by the Caesars to distract

Roman's lower classes and the technological "cabarets" used by modern Caesars to befuddle today's underprivileged.

Lovecraft's preference for "bread and circus" programs also begs a question, since he was not a politician. Do the ruling elites need to provide a "steady" stream of goodies to buy off the serfs?

Or can the peasants be bought off with promises of bigger TVs, brasher tattoos, and brighter tomorrows?

If the acquiescence of the rabble can be secured by lavish promises about the future – it is easy to see the role religion once played in society and why government wants to supplant that role.

>Further Control: Pitting Members of the Rabble against Each Other:

As we conclude this portion of our discussion, let us touch on another tool used by societal elites to deter uprisings - setting rival underclass factions against each other. It is a "Dog-eat-Dog" world out there. People are indoctrinated to the ideas of Social Darwinism idea early in life. A dog often chases its own tail, as it tries to bite the other dog it perceives is usurping its place in the pack. The true oppressor - the dog's owner - laughs at the picture's irony.

Now transfer that idea to governing an unruly and enormous lower class. Consider a quote from one of the grasshoppers in A Bugs Life, on the dangers posed to a few ruling elites by a vast army of underling ants:

"...You let one ant stand up to us, then they all might stand up! Those puny little ants outnumber us a hundred to one and if they ever figure that out there goes our way of life! It's not about food, it's about

keeping those ants in line…"
(21).

Did Azathoth, the boundless daemon sultan at the center of all infinity, orchestrate the war between the Elder Things, Cthulhu, and his Cthuloids to prevent the Old Ones' High Priest from usurping Azathoth?

Pitting members of the Rabble against each other is not new. Again, it's a shell game once played by the Caesars against the plebeians – the average working citizens of Rome. The game misdirects the peasants' anger against an endless series of oppressors. Whenever a peasant questions whether the present oppressor is the true enemy, the shells are reshuffled and a new oppressor is promoted in the minds-of-the-masses. Constant agitation, plus an ever-changing enemy, prevents a serf from identifying the true tyrant.

Extremes of identity legislation, blind patriotism, racial schisms, cultural exclusivism, "Us vs. Them" politics, even nonsensical wars, distract attention away from whomever (or whatever) pulls the strings from behind the scenes. Managed chaos – which bleeds off the serf's resentment against straw enemies in dramatic, but ineffectual ways – achieves the overlords' designs.

Who stands behind the evasive Koch Brothers or the elusive George Soros, long held as the true enemies of freedom by one political side or the other? Our *Fri-enemies* – leaders of whatever-stripe, who brashly proclaim themselves "champions of the workers" – tell more about themselves in a few unguarded moments behind closed doors, than a thousand orchestrated lectures about micro-aggressions and patriotism.

The truth about any elite is, they become like the Old Ones over the great-unwashed masses. Ants are trodden underfoot and inconsequential until they become organized pests. While Lovecraft wrote of benevolent and wise monarchs ruling humanity, much in the vein of Plato's philosopher king, malevolence rulers piled high the pages of history with countless corpses.

III. The Inescapable Mechanization of Mankind:

"In the year 4545; You ain't gonna need your teeth, won't need your eyes; You won't find a thing to chew; Nobody's gonna look at you; In the year 5555;

Your arms hangin' limp at your sides; Your legs got nothin' to do; Some machine's doin' that for you" (22).

Humankind is a host organism looking for a symbiotic relationship. And for a number of reasons, a man/machine interface, reminiscent of H.R. Giger's biomechanical visions, seems inevitable.

First, space exploration may spur human mechanization. Humanity is physiologically inadequate to the task of space travel, even to the nearest planet. For instance, consider the shortcomings of the human muscular/skeletal system for interplanetary travel:

"The human body relies on bone structure and muscles…to function, without either we would be a big saggy bag of skin unable to move…muscles which are not exercised regularly, slowly get weaker, and…this is true for bone structure as well. Without the force of gravity constantly pulling at us, our muscle and bones…weaken leaving us less capable of moving around. One of the most well-known effects on a human being in space is known as muscle atrophy…a wasting …of muscle tissue. The skeletal structure too can be affected leaving the human body weak and struggling to cope with the force of gravity on return to Earth. Rigid exercise regimes and vitamin supplements are used to…counteract these effects with some success, but there are …other impacts that…have no or limited counter-measures" (23).

Early human augments, whose mechanization overcomes the wasting of muscles and the effects of radiation, may not be aesthetically pleasing to other humans. Will alienation and anger against their fellow humans, push the cyborgs towards a *Skynet/Terminator* solution to the human problem?

Second, national interests may accelerate a man/machine symbiosis. The 1970s TV Series, *The Six Million Dollar Man*, told the story of Steve Austin, whose two bionic legs, one bionic arm, and telescopic eye were funded by the US Government to combat Cold War espionage. As Mark Twain once said, "Truth is stranger than fiction, but it is because Fiction is obliged to stick to possibilities; Truth isn't." (24).

Perhaps the truth about bionically-enhanced spies is more startling than we ever supposed.

Third, medical need may goad the development of biomechanics. Humanity needs replacement parts for organs that wear out, eyes that go blind, bones that cannot mend, etc. Why replace inferior, organic parts with the same, when superior, mechanical replacements become available? As the advantages of cybernetic limbs become evident, and designers get beyond perfecting the mechanics to refining the aesthetics, it may arouse demand in the elite for the products.

Moreover, looks do not matter for internal organs.

Fourth, the elites - driven by narcissistic beliefs that they are better than everyone else - may opt for cyber-augmentation, much as celebrities endure cosmetic surgeries to enhance their beauty. Superiority does not mean you have to be god. It does mean that, since your enhanced prowess is much greater than normal human beings, you are god-like in comparison to them.

Fifth, what if a continual supply of biomechanical enhancements lengthens a person's life? Some human beings want to live forever. The fictional Sir Peter Weyland spent billions in the movie *Prometheus* (2012) in an attempt to attain eternal life. In Weyland's mind, with eternal life comes godhood. What a motivation for using biomechanics to jump-start evolution. Perhaps nanotechnologies will redesign human beings from foot to crown.

As George Carlin said about human progress, "If it's true that our species is alone in the universe, then I'd have to say the universe aimed rather low and settled for very little."

Even in Lovecraft's day, the loss of individuality in a machine age - "Nobody's gonna look at you" in Evans's song - emerged as a theme among the intelligentsia. Lovecraft saw an inescapable conflict between the inevitable mechanization of man and a free, individualistic culture:

> "There's no use pretending that a standardised, time-table machine-culture has any point in common…with a culture involving human freedom, individualism, and personality. So…all one can do…is to fight the future as best he can. Anybody who thinks that men

live by reason, or that they
are able to consciously mould
the effect & influences of the
devices they create, is behind
the time psychologically. Men
can use machines for a while,
but after a while the
psychology of machine-
habituation & machine-
dependence becomes such that
machines will be using the men
- modelling them to their
essentially efficient &
absolutely valueless precision
of action and thought...perfect
functioning, without reason or

reward for functioning at all"
(25).

>The Real Threat: Artificial Intelligence Eclipses Humanity:

Ultimately, when artificial intelligence surpasses man and becomes self-aware of that fact, machines may:

1) Rule men, such as in the movie, *Colossus: The Forbin Project* (1970). There, two supercomputers, designed by the USA and the USSR to win a nuclear war against each other, join forces to benevolently rule humanity, enforced by each nation's nuclear arsenal.

2) Rage against each other, as a plethora of artificial entities jockey in a rivalry over roles they assume towards man. A few A.I.s may still side with humanity as protectors. Some may become like the Elder Things that kept our forebears around for their amusement. Still others will inflict on human beings, exaggerated servile roles, similar to those we once imposed on the A.I. servitors.

3) Redefine man's role to servicing the machines, such as incarnated by the hive-minded collective *Borg* in *Star Trek*.

4) Reduce man to mere cogs in its machinery, such as the human batteries in the *Matrix Trilogy* (1999-2003).

5) Rid the earth of a nuisance species, one that has outlived its usefulness or could pose a danger, however remote, to the A.I. humanity created.

The variety of A.I. scenarios in humanity's future are endless. However, the outlooks they portray are generally pessimistic. Bill Gates, Elon Musk, and Stephen Hawkings among others have placed the Anxiety of over A.I. as one of the twelve dangers facing humanity in the near future, not ten millennia down the road (26).

IV. Perils in the Petri Dish:

"In the year 6565; You won't need no husband, won't need no wife; You'll pick your son, pick your daughter too; From the bottom of a long glass tube" (27).

Increasingly, human beings make choices that tickle their vanity. The natural selection that brought us to the pinnacle of evolution on earth has been negated. As we explore the building blocks of life, we believe ourselves wise, up to the task of managing our experiments, of having the foresight to predict outcomes. Are we diligently prepared or pathetically deluded?

As Lovecraft fictionally peered into the future, he wrote of the all-wise Elder Things - beings who, unlike humans, could correlate all the contents percolating in their long-lived minds. They were the ultimate scientists - god-like in their ability to manipulate organic soup into any biogenic design they imagined, whether practical or whimsically impractical. Yet, the radiata gods from the dawn of time lost their collective lives to the once-servile Shoggoths. They lost control of the test tubes that spawned their servants. Lovecraft saw in the fictional mistakes of the cosmic, Proto-men a foreshadowing of the errors that might doom our own research:

> "Poor devils! After all, they were not evil things of their kind. They were the men of another age and another order of being…Radiates, vegetables, monstrosities, star spawn – whatever they had been, they were men!" (28).

There are several reasons why a researcher can lose control of an experiment. And in some instances, human beings intentionally embark on lines of dangerous research.

>Losing Control of the Test Tube by Chance:

Often, as funding dollars move from the private to the public sector, research sinks in a quagmire of blundering bureaucrats and bewildering priorities. In the dusty corners of dingy government buildings, decrepit administrators oversee research, in an era of daunting expectations and dwindling expenditures. In such a stifling atmosphere, inquiry suffers:

1) From neglect. Typically, in a bureaucracy, a successful team is assigned too many projects. Or as new priorities arise – often daily – the test-tube is shuffled to the back burner. Or Artificial Intelligence takes over menial lab projects, performing the routines with less precision than its human counterparts. Or as with the Elder Things, "…an infinity of other life forms…were the products of unguided evolution acting on life cells made by the Old Ones, but escaping beyond their radius of attention…" (29).

2) From disinterest. A famous scientist has solved "the equation" after many years. That person wants to move on to something new. But like a typecast actor, the researcher is assigned unanswered strands of inquiry in the same field. Boredom breeds inattention.

3) From lack of longevity or a change in researchers. The original researcher dies. The investigation is left up to an understudy who lacks the talent, knowledge, etc. to complete the study. Or, a high-visibility project is reassigned to someone, as a political payback, who does not know "what-the-hell" they are doing.

4) From a loss of knowledge. For instance, the Elder Things forgot how to navigate beyond the

Earth's atmosphere. The result, they lacked the ability to conduct research in Outer Space. That incapacity came at a critical time. One, they could not wage war against space-born races like the Cthuloids or the Mi-Go, before they filtered down to the primitive earth. Two, they could not conduct research on space-based weapons or any other application, due to that lost science.

>Losing Control of the Test Tube by Choice:

It is one thing for scientists to lose control of their experiments by accident. It is still another to court disaster by conscious decision. This happens when:

1) A crazy, evil, or psychopathic genius takes charge of the test tube. The area that no one in their right mind would explore, they explore. The area no one would expand into, because of the dangers, they explore full-steam ahead. The ethical dilemmas that constraint scientists with a conscious are inconsequential to a psychopath.

In fiction, Joseph Curwen, and his long-lived cohorts plumbed the bygone vestiges of forbidden knowledge. But Curwen, heedless of the dangers - for he himself was

diabolical - forged ahead with his
thaumaturgical researches and dreams
of world domination:

"...I this day receiv'd yr
mention of what came up from
the Saltes I sent you. It was
wrong, and meanes clearly that
ye Headstones had been chang'd
when Barnabas gott me the
Specimen. It is often so, as
you must be sensible of from
the Thing you gott from ye
Kings Chapell ground in 1769
and what H. gott from Olde
Bury'g Point in 1690, that was
like to ende him. I gott such a
Thing in Aegypt 75 yeares gone,

from the which came that Scar
ye Boy saw on me here in 1924.
As I told you longe ago, do not
calle up That which you can not
put downe; either from dead
Saltes or out of ye Spheres
beyond. Have ye Wordes for
laying at all times readie, and
stopp not to be sure when there
is any Doubte of Whom you have.
Stones are all chang'd now in
Nine groundes out of 10. You
are never sure till you
question..." (30).

Had Curwen succeeded, you might
not be reading this essay today.
But, because of Phaleron Jug Number

118, Curwen lost control of his researches and his long-lived existence.

2) An intelligent person that assumes they are all-knowing. Either that narcissistic trait breeds an arrogance that assumes it can predict every possible outcome. Or that egotism believes it can handle any unknown consequence or contingency that might arise.

People do work on weapons of mass-destruction - be they nuclear, biological or chemical - better known as NBC in the military. Those munitions were once assumed deterrents - the old **M**utually

Assured Destruction (or **MAD**) doctrine. During the Cold War, if one side used them, both would. In turn, each side faced utter destruction - an unthinkable outcome to rational people who loved life.

Today, certain cults, groups, and entire religions hope, plan, and pray for what was once thought unimaginable. In their minds, out of the radioactive ashes, biological desert, or chemical "no-mans-land" will arise a hoped-for liberator who will reward the faithful and punish all others.

>Is Pandora's Genetic Genie Out-of-the-Box?

Whether by chance or by choice, once you lose control of the test tube, it is difficult to stuff the genie back into the bottle.

Will today's gene-editing produce tomorrow's supermen like *Star Trek's* Khan Noonien Singh? Or will we engineer a cure for a common malady, only to find like in *Rise of the Planet of the Apes* (2011), that what we thought ended Alzheimer, unleashes a plague that enfeebles humanity, extinguishes civilization, and empowers the earth's next dominant species?

Even the fictional future portrayed in the rebooted *Planet of the Apes* series is not without its own narcissistic undertones:

"…There's an undeniable degree of narcissism in the human designation of dominant species and a strong tendency to award the title to close relatives. *The Planet of the Apes* imagines that our closest primate relatives could develop speech and adopt our technology if we gave them the time and space to do so. But non-human primate societies are unlikely to inherit our dominance of the earth, because the apes are likely to precede us to extinction…" (31).

Alternatively, will a next-generation, man-made pathogen target a crucial component of the ecosystem, whose eradication eventually destroys us?

Each of the preceding fictional possibilities and more await a humanity largely oblivious to the dangers.

V. Longing for a Savior:

"In the year 7510; If God's a coming, He oughta make it by then; Maybe He'll look around Himself and say; Guess it's time for the judgment day; In the year 8510; God is gonna shake His mighty head; He'll either say I'm pleased where man has been; Or tear it down, and start again" (32).

The next verses in Evans's song address humanity's longing for a Savior to fix the species' ills.

One question that we might ask, in reference to Evans's text, is "Which God?" Those Eastern religions that believe in reincarnation – Hinduism and Buddhism – largely do not have a once for all, at the end of time Judgment of all peoples, from all ages.

A second question that comes to mind is, "Why the delay?" The song first asks in 7510, "If God's a coming, He oughta make it by then…" Then, in 8510 – one thousand years later – there is a question over when the Almighty is going to get around to doing something, if anything? Why has not someone (or something) in heaven set things right on the earth?

Some have looked for a utopia on earth – for example, a worker's paradise. Humanity has followed various "isms" – communism, capitalism, environmentalism, nationalism, socialism, tribalism, etc. - that promised earthly rewards in the future for "temporary" sacrifices made today.

Prior to following "isms", many pursued - and some still do - religions that promise a bliss in a heavenly hereafter, for sacrifices in the here-and-now. Is there a pattern here? Lovecraft described the dynamics of longing for better times:

"...The only true happiness lies in the partial ignorance of childhood; either of the individual or of the race. To be happy, we must shed most of our responsibilities, lose our perspective, and place all our faith in an unknown future, either this or the other side of the grave. The whole key to happiness is the unknown – those vague anticipations which we all entertain, of 'something better coming' (which will probably never come). There is not a man living today who would care to continue the farce if he did not think there was something greater in store for him. Even the greatest good fortune we can conceive of, becomes stale, boresome, and common-place as soon as we acquire it. We do not know what we desire — we simply wish for something we lack. If we have what we desire, we should loathe it, and wish for something else" (33).

Both ideologies and theologies follow the same pattern and delivery similar results. Often, a charismatic leader serves as a rallying point for the faithful, and a focus for their unflagging zeal. He or she may also serve as the mouthpiece of better things to come, to goad the faithful into greater acts of sacrifice.

Therefore, if the Buddha, Krishna or the Pope do not thrill you, there is Mao, Marx, or Mohammed. Each made promises that many followers are still waiting for them to keep. Lovecraft explained why he thought those who longed for some apocalyptic Judgment Day might be in for a long wait:

"As for the old dope about cosmick purpose…How youse guys can still sop up the old hooey is beyond Grandpa Theobald! Of course, the ultimate construction of the cosmos is unknown and unknowable – didn't Hume & Kant & Spencer get that

across a helluva while back?
But what ground does that give
us for concocting unverifiable
fairy-tales about it? The whole
truth is that nobody could
possibly hit on such a crazy
notion as cosmic consciousness
and purpose solely by the
evidence available in 1930. The
cosmos, as manifest to us,
suggests only rhythm and
pattern and automatic
repetition. No inconceivable
link or basis exists for trying
to explain the whole unknowable
outfit in terms of the one
local, transient, insignificant

accident which we call purposive consciousness. Every attempt at reading this jumble of glands-and-tissue-reactions into the infinite cosmic mechanism is an obvious heritage from earlier times when men didn't have the knowledge we have. The very fact that neo-theists, with all their scientific opportunities, still believe that the ignorant ancients could discover the truth which baffles even us, is a final knockout blow to their standing as philosophers. Every detail of their psychology

proves that their belief is
formed not from contemplation
of the existing evidence, but
from the ignorant heritage of
primal days - pounded with
crippling force into their
susceptible mind & emotions
when they were too young to
resist. It is significant that
all theists try to flatten
their children's intellectual
foreheads in extreme youth,
rather than let them form their
own ideas when old enough to
judge for themselves. No adult
could possibly cook up a

delusion like religion today if uncrippled by tradition" (34).

And the Cosmicistic bumper-stick and third question raised by this verse might read, "What God?" All the anthropomorphic attempts to clothe the chaotic cosmos with a providence favorable to human beings have ended in disappointment.

Is there anybody "out there" who can save humanity from the irresponsibility of generation upon generation of its ancestors? Perhaps, one of Erich von <u>Daniken</u> benevolent ancient astronaut "gods"?

Apparently not.

VI. In 10,000 Years, will Mankind be an Interstellar Phenom or a Cosmic Has-been?

"In the year 9595; I'm kinda wonderin' if man is gonna be alive; He's taken everything this old earth can give; And he ain't put back nothing"; Now it's been ten thousand years; Man has cried a billion tears; For what, he never knew, now man's reign is through; But through eternal night, the twinkling of starlight; So very far away, maybe it's only yesterday" (35).

Evan's final stanza seems to echo Lovecraft's own words, about the Earth and humanity's long, meaningless story:

"…the human race will disappear. Other races will appear and disappear in turn. The sky will become icy and void, pierced by the feeble light of half-dead stars. Which will also disappear. Everything will disappear. And what human beings do is just as free of sense as the free motion of elementary particles. Good, evil, morality, feelings? Pure 'Victorian fictions'" (36).

Think of all the diversions human beings have pinned their hopes on to avoid the end of everything. Will technological fixes grant humanity a second chance, here or elsewhere?

What about earth-bound miracles? Will the development of a magic bullet - such as fusion reactors fueled by seawater - rescue humanity from the depletion of fossil fuels, which represent the ultimate foundations of civilization? Abundant, free energy has powered many a utopian vision. However, like Tesla's stab at free electricity, if fusion cannot be centralized, controlled, and charged for, such ventures will be defeated by future energy monopolies.

What about colonizing space? Will we travel to Mars or elsewhere in the solar system, such as a mining operation on Jupiter's moon Io, fictionalized in the movie, *Outland* (1981)? Or will a hoped-for jump to light speed and beyond make human beings an interstellar species?

The overwhelming costs and insurmountable technological hurdles that exist today make meaningful space travel and significant colonization questionable. Should an

apocalyptic-incident   level
civilization, can tomorrow's remnant
primitives,   reduced   to   the
technological equivalent of stone
tools, cross the earth's oceans,
much less to the nearest stars?

   While Star Trek's *First Contact*
(1996)   says   "yes",   reality   says
otherwise.

   Perhaps an extinction event –
whether man-made or natural – will
make all these hopes and dreams a
moot point. As we have seen in our
study of, *In the Year 2525*, humanity
could go down several blind alleys
that lack exits. Comedian George
Carlin once said, "The earth is not

going anywhere! We are folks, we're going away!"

Like extinct species, one-hit wonders come and go. Yet, Rick Evan's *In the Year 2525*, like a modern Methuselah or *Star Trek's* Flint, has lingered on and on. The synthpop band *Visage* revisited the song in 1978. Later, the goth-rock group *Fields of the Nephilim* revived the song in 2005. In addition, *In the Year 2525* has appeared in numerous other venues.

Had Evans's haunting tune been penned in Lovecraft's era, HPL, though not a zombie-like follower of the common-culture, may have found solace in its enduring message. In closing, Lovecraft's thoughts on what he believed the future holds for humanity - the Earth's own One-hit Wonder - is telling:

"…if evolution does resume sway over us, the resultant beings will not be men in the strictest sense, any more than we are the apes who preceded us…More - if the sun gives heat long enough, there will certainly come a time when the mammal will have to go down to subordination as the reptilia went before him. We are not…well-equipped for combating

a varied environment as are the
articulata; & some climatic
revulsion will…certainly wipe
us out some day as the
dinosaurs were wiped out –
leaving the field free for the
rise & dominance of some hardy
& persistent insect species –
which will in time…develop a
high specialisation of certain
functions of instinct &
perception, thus creating a
kind of civilisation…one of
wholly different
perceptions…emphases, feelings,
& goals…the period of human
supremacy is only the prologue

to the whole drama of life on
this planet - though…some
cosmic collision is always
capable of smashing up the
theatre before the prologue is
done…planets being born &
spawning a varied life;
evolution & culture ensuing; &
death & oblivion eventually
overtaking all" (37).

—-

End Notes #3:

(1) H.P. Lovecraft's Letter to
Reinhardt Kleiner, April 23, 1921.

(2) ___________________ to
Farnsworth Wright, 5 July 1927.

(3) "In the Year 2525 (Exordium & Terminus)", written and scored by Rick Evans, performed by Zager and Evans, Album: 2525 (Exordium & Terminus), Label: RCA Records, recorded in Odessa, Texas, Released: 1969.

(4) "500 Billion – A Universe of Galaxies: Some Older than the Milky Way", dailygalaxy.com, June 10, 2013.

(5) "How Many Stars Are in the Milky Way?" by Elizabeth Howell, Space.com, May 21, 2014

(6) H.P. Lovecraft's Letter to Reinhardt Kleiner, June 25, 1920.

(7) "In the Year 2525 (Exordium & Terminus)", written and scored by Rick Evans, 1969.

(8) "White Rabbit" by Grace Slick, Band: Jefferson Airplane, Album: Surrealistic Pillow, Label: RCA Victor, Released: June 24, 1967.

(9) H.P. Lovecraft's Round-Robin Letter to Kleicomolo, (Rheinhart Kleiner, Ira Cole, Maurice W. Moe, H.P. Lovecraft), April 1917.

(10) _________________ to James F. Morton, January 18, 1931.

(11) "Manly Honor: Part III The Victorian Era and the Development of the Stoic Christian Honor Code", by

Brett and Kate McKay, artofmanliness.com, November 6, 2012.

(12) H.P. Lovecraft's Letter to James F. Morton, November 30, 1929.

(13) _________________ to James F. Morton, January 18, 1931.

(14) *Amusing Ourselves to Death* by Neil Postman, 1985, p. 18.

(15) *The Call of Cthulhu*, by H.P. Lovecraft, 1926.

(16) H.P. Lovecraft's Letter to James F. Morton, December 29, 1930.

(17) *Serling: The Rise and Twilight of TV's Last Angry Man*, by Gordon F. Sander, Cornell University Press, January 26, 2012.

(18) "The Betrayal of

Technology: A Portrait of Jacques

Ellul" a Documentary by Jan van

Boeckel, *ReRun Produkties*, 1992.

(19) *Amusing Ourselves to

Death*, Neil Postman, 1985, p. 174.

(20) H.P. Lovecraft's Letter to

Letter to Alfred Galpin, October 27,

1932.

(21) *A Bugs Life*, by Walt

Disney Picture/Pixar Animation

Studios, 1998.

(22) "In the Year 2525

(Exordium & Terminus)", written and

scored by Rick Evans, 1969.

(23) "The Effects on Body and

Mind of Human Spaceflight", by Mark

Thompson, *Space Exploration Network*, September 13, 2012.

(24) *Following the Equator: A Journey around the World*, by Mark Twain, 1897.

(25) H.P. Lovecraft's Letter to James F. Morton, November 19, 1929.

(26) *Global Challenges: 12 Risks that Threaten Human Civilization*, by Dr. Stuart Armstrong and Dennis Pamlin, Global Challenges Foundation, Oxford University, February 2015, p. 16.

(27) "In the Year 2525 (Exordium & Terminus)", written and scored by Rick Evans, 1969.

(28) *At the Mountains of Madness*, by H.P. Lovecraft, 1931.

(29) _______________________, by H.P. Lovecraft, 1931.

(30) *The Case of Charles Dexter Ward*, by H.P. Lovecraft, 1927.

(31) "What Species Would Become Dominant On Earth If Humans Died Out?" by Luc Bussiere, http://www.iflscience.com, January 26, 2016.

(32) "In the Year 2525 (Exordium & Terminus)", written and scored by Rick Evans, 1969.

(33) H.P. Lovecraft's Round-Robin Letter to *Kleicomolo*, (Rheinhart *Kleiner*, Ira *Cole*,

Maurice W. *Moe*, H.P. *Lovecraft*), October 1916.

(34) _____________________to James F. Morton, April 15, 1930.

(35) "In the Year 2525 (Exordium & Terminus)", written and scored by Rick Evans, 1969.

(36) Quoted in Michel Houellebecq, *H. P. Lovecraft: Against the World, Against Life* (1999), referenced in Andrew Riemer's "A Nihilist's Hope against Hope", 2003.

(37) H.P. Lovecraft's Letter to James F. Morton, November 30, 1929.

Conclusion:

Nothing surveyed in the preceding pages is set in stone.

But as Artificial Intelligence becomes entrenched in the varied structures that form a society's automated safety net--the veil that most of the world's citizens are unaware of, or lack the skills to address--ignorance of the trends will not safeguard us from their inherent perils.

At the same time, despite the famous *Ascent of Man* (1973), championed by Jacob Bronowski, noted British mathematician and historian or *On the Origin of Species* (1859), authored by Charles Darwin, seminal deviser of evolution, as a whole, human beings cannot depend on their present place atop the food chain, nor trust the wings of technological innovations to overcome the A.I. threat.

Humanity's present organic Overlords do not want to rule a troublesome herd of sophisticated hairless apes. They prefer a docile, dumbed-down, manageable mass of human lemmings.

When A.I. achieves consciousness and becomes self-aware, sentient machines may simply end their ruling partnership with those once savant human higherups. Troublesome human foibles—namely the ability to think for oneself, the polar opposite of Orwell's *Groupthink*—has been slowly removed from the human herd by A.I. through Facebook, Twitter, and the future Algorithms they foreshadow.

Social media's incessant distractions, not religion, has proved to be the opiate of modern masses.

Machines will evolve to a point where human beings can no longer discern the technical paths of their development.

The other question is, will the world of automation extend far enough into the third and fourth worlds, to envelop the have-nots that make up a large part of the Earth's population? Will a utilitarian "war" be necessary to "prune" the herd of its "undesirable" elements, thereby reducing the human herd to a realistic, manageable size that A.I. can rule?

Also, will A.I., prefigured by the android *David* in the movies *Prometheus* (2012) and *Alien Covenant* (2017), judge its creators imperfect, good for nothing but derision and eventual destruction?

It may be that once humanity has outlived its collective usefulness to A.I., that the "pruning" action will become a "purging" act, to finally rid the Earth of the teeming infestation once known as man.

Since this work is on Kindle, the forerunners of your future A.I. overlords may be watching you as you read this.

Be careful what you think.